First World War
and Army of Occupation
War Diary
France, Belgium and Germany

16 DIVISION
48 Infantry Brigade
Princess Victoria's (Royal Irish Fusiliers)
5th Battalion
1 May 1918 - 9 June 1919

WO95/1975/1

The Naval & Military Press Ltd
www.nmarchive.com
Published in association with The National Archives

Published by

The Naval & Military Press Ltd

Unit 10 Ridgewood Industrial Park,

Uckfield, East Sussex,

TN22 5QE England

Tel: +44 (0) 1825 749494

www.naval-military-press.com

www.nmarchive.com

This diary has been reprinted in facsimile from the original. Any imperfections are inevitably reproduced and the quality may fall short of modern type and cartographic standards.

© Crown Copyright
Images reproduced by permission of The National Archives, London, England, 2015.

Contents

Document type	Place/Title	Date From	Date To
Heading	1975/1 1918 May-1919 June 5 Battalion Royal Irish Fusiliers		
Heading	16 Div 48 Inf Bde 5 Bn. Roy. Ir. Fus. 48 Bde 16th Div. May 5 June 1918 21. Bde 30th Div 16/25 June 1918 L of C 26th June-21st July 198th Bde 66 Div 22nd July-23rd Aug 48 Bde 16th-Div 24th Aug May 1918-June 1919 From Egypt 10 Div 31 Bde		
Heading	War Diary of 5th (S) Bn Royal Irish Fusiliers from 1/5/18 to 31/5/18 Vol No 36 Pages 1-203. Vol 1		
War Diary	Khurbetha Ibn Harith	01/05/1918	01/05/1918
War Diary	Latron	02/05/1918	02/05/1918
War Diary	Ludd	03/05/1918	04/05/1918
War Diary	Kantara	05/05/1918	18/05/1918
War Diary	Port Said	19/05/1918	27/05/1918
War Diary	Marseilles	28/05/1918	31/05/1918
Heading	War Diary of 5th (S) Bn Royal Irish Fusiliers from 1/6/18 to 30/6/18 Vol No 37 Pages 1 to 3 Vol 2		
War Diary		01/06/1918	03/06/1918
War Diary	Manqueville	04/06/1918	16/06/1918
War Diary	Monchaux	17/06/1918	20/06/1918
War Diary	Canchy.	21/06/1918	27/06/1918
War Diary	Les Hauts Chenes	28/06/1918	30/06/1918
Heading	War Diary Of 5th (Service) Bn Royal Irish Fus., From-July 1st To-July 31st 1918 Vol XXXVIII.		
War Diary	Abancourt	01/07/1918	22/07/1918
War Diary	Haudricourt	23/07/1918	31/07/1918
Miscellaneous	B.M. 32/7	02/09/1918	02/09/1918
Heading	War Diary of 5th (S) Bn R. Irish Fus From 1st Aug to 31st Aug. 1918 (Vol. No 39)		
War Diary	Haudricourt	01/08/1918	24/08/1918
War Diary	Bois D'Olhain	25/08/1918	27/08/1918
War Diary	Noeux Les Mines.	27/08/1918	29/08/1918
War Diary	Barlin	30/08/1918	31/08/1918
Heading	War Diary Of 5th R. Irish Fusiliers From 1st September to 30th September 1918 Vol No 40		
War Diary	Barlin	01/09/1918	06/09/1918
War Diary	Noeux Les Mines.	07/09/1918	18/09/1918
War Diary	Annequin	19/09/1918	27/09/1918
War Diary	In The Line	28/09/1918	30/09/1918
Heading	War Diary of 5th (S) Bn. Royal Irish Fusiliers From 1st October. 1918 To 31st October. 1918. Volume No 41		
War Diary	In The Line	01/10/1918	01/10/1918
War Diary	Cambrin	02/10/1918	03/10/1918
War Diary	Braddell Point	04/10/1918	04/10/1918
War Diary	Robertson's Tunnel	05/10/1918	09/10/1918
War Diary	Cambrin	10/10/1918	15/10/1918
War Diary	Cite De Douvrin.	15/10/1918	15/10/1918
War Diary	Billy	16/10/1918	16/10/1918
War Diary	Provin	17/10/1918	17/10/1918
War Diary	Attiches	18/10/1918	21/10/1918

War Diary	Ennevlin	22/10/1918	31/10/1918
Heading	War Diary Of 5th (S.) Bn. Royal Irish Fusiliers. From 1st Nov. 1918 To 30th Nov. 1918 Volume No. 42		
War Diary	Ennevelin	01/11/1918	03/11/1918
War Diary	Rumes	04/11/1918	06/11/1918
War Diary	In The Line	07/11/1918	10/11/1918
War Diary	Antoing	11/11/1918	14/11/1918
War Diary	Line of March.	15/11/1918	16/11/1918
War Diary	Merignies Area K 6 12, L 1.7	17/11/1918	27/11/1918
War Diary	Merignies	28/11/1918	29/11/1918
War Diary	Templeuve	30/11/1918	30/11/1918
Heading	War Diary of 5th (S) Bn Royal Irish Fusiliers From 1st Dec 1918 to 31st Dec. 1918 Volume No 43 Pages 1-2		
War Diary	Templeuve	01/12/1918	31/12/1918
Heading	War Diary of 5th (S). Bn. Royal Irish Fusiliers. From January 1st 1919 to January 31st 1919 Volume 44		
War Diary	Templeuve	01/01/1919	31/01/1919
Heading	War Diary of 5th (S). Bn Royal Irish Fusiliers From February 1st 1919 to February 28th 1919 Volume No 45		
War Diary	Templeuve	01/02/1919	28/02/1919
Heading	War Diary of 5th (S). Bn Royal Irish Fusiliers from March 1st 1919 to March 31st 1919 Volume No 46		
War Diary	Templeuve	01/03/1919	31/03/1919
Heading	War Diary of 5th (S) Bn Royal Irish Fusiliers from 1st April 1919 to 30th April 1919 Volume No 47		
War Diary	Templeuve (Nord)	01/04/1919	30/04/1919
Heading	War Diary of 5th (S) Bn. Royal Irish Fusiliers. from 1/5/19 to 31/5/19 Volume No 48		
War Diary	Templeuve (Nord)	01/05/1919	31/05/1919
Heading	War Diary Of 5th (S.) Bn. Royal Irish Fusiliers from 1st June 1919 to 9th June 1919. Vol. 49		
War Diary	Mardyck	01/06/1919	03/06/1919
War Diary	Southampton	04/06/1919	05/06/1919
War Diary	Georgetown	06/06/1919	06/06/1919
War Diary	Prees Heath	07/06/1919	07/06/1919
War Diary	Belfast	08/06/1919	09/06/1919

1975/1

1918 June – 1919 June
   May

5 Battalion Royal Irish Fusiliers

16 DIV
48 INF BDE

5ᵗʰ Bn. Roy. Ir. Fus.
? 48 Bde 16° Div. (May & June 1918)
? 21° Bde 30° Div (16/25 June 1918)
? L of C. 26ᵗʰ June – 21ˢᵗ July
198° Bde 66 Div 22ⁿᵈ July – 23ʳᵈ Aug
48 Bde 16ᵗʰ Div 24ᵗʰ Aug –

France

May 1918 — June 1919

FROM EGYPT 10 DIV. 31 BDE

1978

No 1 48/76

S.20

Confidential
War Diary
of
5th (S) Bn Royal Irish Fusiliers
From 1/5/18 to 31/5/18
Vol No 36

Pages 1-203

WAR DIARY or INTELLIGENCE SUMMARY

Army Form C. 2118

Vol. 36 Page 1

Place	Date May	Hour	Summary of Events and Information	Remarks and references to Appendices
KHURBETHA IBN HARITH	1st		Battalion moved at dusk to LATRON.	
LATRON	2nd		" " " " SURAFEND Camp, LUDD	
LUDD	3rd		Resting.	
	4th		Battalion entrained at LUDD Station at 1300, detraining 1445.	
KANTARA	5th		Battalion detrains 0630 and marches to camp at Kilo 5 on DUEIDAR ROAD. Kit inspection to Coy. battn. in afternoon. Lieut. R.J.Sharp awarded Croix de Guerre. Cpl O'Connor "health pistol" reported from hospital.	
	6th		Company training. Lt.Col. 2nd Lt. Johnson rejoined from hospital and resumed Command; hospitalised resuming duties of Second in Command, and Capt. W.S. Sweeting commanding "D" Coy. Lieut. G.C. Kirkland joined, posted to "A" Coy. 2/Lt. H.W. Munro " " " "B" Coy. 2/Lt. R.J. Madden " " " "C" Coy. Short leave in Egypt opens.	
	7th			
	8th		Company training. Capt. A.R. Jenkin Caza returned from staff Course at 31 Ey.f.Div.	
	9th		Advance party from QUI-store Transport, Horses & ALEXANDRIA Kran equipment. Disinfection of battalion. Draft of 99 O.Rs. rejoined.	

WAR DIARY or INTELLIGENCE SUMMARY

Title: 5 R. Irish Rgt. Vol. 36 Page 2

Place	Date	Hour	Summary of Events and Information	Remarks and references to Appendices
KANTARA	10th		Company training, bathing &c.	
	11th		" " " "	
	12th		Divine Service; Capt. S. P.C. Lawes addresses by Capt. K. R. MacDonald.	
	13th		Company training, bathing &c. Washing, by Coys. 2 ORs rejoined from hospital.	
	14th		Washing. Firing on Kantara Rifle Range.	
	15th		Baking. " " " " 19 ORs rejoined from hospital.	
	16th		" " " " " Capt. Wakeattie M.C. rejoined from hospital & resumed Command of "C" Coy. Lieut. A.H. James joined (commissioned from the ranks 2nd Connaught Rangers) for duty. Posted to "B" Coy. Lt. W.P. Dickson appointed Capt. Adjt.	
	17th		Lieut. J. Arnott rejoined from hospital. Draft of 10 ORs rejoined.	
	18th		Battalion entrained 0850, arriving at Port Said at 1020. Transport embarked at KANTARA. Embarked on H.M.T. "Huntspill".	

Army Form C. 2118

WAR DIARY
or
INTELLIGENCE SUMMARY

5 R. Irish Dns. Vol 36. Page 3.

(Erase heading not required.)

Place	Date May.	Hour	Summary of Events and Information	Remarks and references to Appendices
Port SAID	19th		Battalion sails at 0700.	
	20th		Calm weather.	
	21st		" "	
	22nd		" "	
	23rd		" "	
	24th		Cloudy.	
	25th		" "	
	26th		Calm weather.	
	27th		Battalion arrived at MARSEILLES at 1700 and disembarked 1900; marched to No.10 Rest Camp. Transport arrived same evening.	
MARSEILLES	28th		Settling in.	
	29th		Company Drawing, Pro drill, Arms drill rc.	
	30th		Battalion route march.	
	31st		Battalion entrained at 07.27 at MARSEILLES.	

J. W. E. Johnson Lt Col
Comd 5 R Ir Fus

Confidential
War Diary
of
5(S) Bn Royal Irish Fusiliers
From 1/6/18 to 30/6/18
Vol No 37
Pages 1 to 3.

Army Form C. 2118

WAR DIARY
or
INTELLIGENCE SUMMARY

(Erase heading not required.)

5th R. Irish Fus. Vol. 37. Page 1.

Place	Date	Hour	Summary of Events and Information	Remarks and references to Appendices
	1st June		Train journey continued. Halts at PARAY LE MONIAL and MALESHERBES.	
	2nd		" " " US and ABBEVILLE.	
	3rd		" " concluded. Battalion detrained (34 offrs. 834 O.Rs) at AIRE 0830	France
			and marched to MANQUEVILLE. A + B in billets, C + D under canvas.	36A. U.3.B.8.6.
MANQUEVILLE	4th		Kit inspection.	
	5th		C + D Coy. vacates billets in HAM-en-ARTOIS.	
	6th		Trench digging on LILLERS — STEENBECQUE.	
	7th		" " " Q.M. rejoined with equipment.	
	8th		Bathing at LA LACQUE.	
	9th		Chisel handles R.E. + Continues Reg I. Rec.	
	10th		Work on line.	
	11th		Inspection by Corps Commander. Gas lecture throwing through Gas	
	12th		Work on line.	
	13th		" "	
	14th		" " Capt. A.G. Potts to Hospital	

WAR DIARY or INTELLIGENCE SUMMARY

Army Form C. 2118

Vol. 37 Page 2

5th R. Innis. Fus. (Erase heading not required.)

Place	Date	Hour	Summary of Events and Information	Remarks and references to Appendices
	15th		Battalion marched to AIRE Station & entrained at 1600, leaving at 1700.	
	16th		Battalion detrained at LONGROY-GAMACHES and marched to MONCHAUX.	Dieppe 1/100,000
MONCHAUX	17th		Settling in: Kit inspections v.c. Lt.Col. J.S.T.Johnson D.S.O. assumed command 37th Inf. Bde.	
	18th		Company training. Major R.R. French assumed command of the Bn.	
	19th		Battalion marches from MONCHAUX to BEHEN.	Abbeville 1/100,000
	20th		— — BEHEN to CANCHY.	
CANCHY	21st		Kit inspections &c.	
	22nd		Medical inspection for Malaria by Lt.Col. DALRYMPLE and A.D.M.S. 30th Div. Rev. W.J. CARROLL M.C. joined. Capt. R. McEWAN rejoined from leave to U.K.	
	23rd		Church Parade, R.C. only. 2/Lt. M.J. ARLOTT transferred to "B" Coy.	
	24th		A Coy. bathing. Remainder: Training, Platoon training & specialist classes. Lieut. J.H. DOLAN to hospital. Lt. J.L. CREIGHTON joined from U.K. and posted to B Coy. 2/Lt. H.A. J. BERRY — — — A — 2/Lt. P.J.T. CATER — — — D —	
	25th		Coy. training.	
	26th		Battalion entrained at ABBEVILLE, leaving at 2000.	
	27th		Battalion detrained at FORGES-LES-EAUX at 0300 & marched to LES HAUTECHENES.	Dieppe 1/100,000

1875 Wt. W593/826 1,000,000 4/15 J.B.C. & A. A.D.S.S./Forms/C. 2118.

Army Form C. 2118

WAR DIARY
or
INTELLIGENCE SUMMARY

(Erase heading not required.)

5 R Irish Fus   Vol. 37   Page 3

Place	Date	Hour	Summary of Events and Information	Remarks and references to Appendices
LES HAUTS CHENES	Sept 29th		Company training. Fatigue parties supplies to Camp. No parade tomorrow. Church parade. R.C.	Scoffe 1/100,000
	30th			

b/ Nichoo

M Deveron Major

CONFIDENTIAL — Vol III

WAR DIARY

OF

5th (Service) Bn Royal Irish Fus.,

FROM :- July 1st TO :- July 31st
1918

— VOL XXXVIII —

Transferred to 16 Div in Aug.

S.22

Army Form C. 2118

WAR DIARY
or
INTELLIGENCE SUMMARY

(Erase heading not required.)

Vol. 38 Page 1

Instructions regarding War Diaries and Intelligence Summaries are contained in F.S. Regs., Part II. and the Staff Manual respectively. Title Pages 2 R. Irish Regt. will be prepared in manuscript.

Place	Date	Hour	Summary of Events and Information	Remarks and references to Appendices
July	1st.		Battalion marched to vicinity of ABANCOURT. Rev. W.J. Cannon M.C. left to join 30 Div. Lt. F.S. Simpson joined unit from 3rd Bn. R. Ir. Div.	Dieppe 16 1/100,000
ABANCOURT	2(d)-		Construction of Anti-aircraft trenches	
	3rd-		Training under company arrangements	
	4th-		Lieut. T.H. Dolan rejoined from Hospital	
	5th-		Training interfered by epidemic of influenza.	
	6th-		Coy. training.	
	7th-		-	
	8th-		- Draft of 43 ORs rejoined from hospital	
	9th-		- - 12 - -	
	10th-		Capt. & Rev. J. CAMPBELL to hospital. 2/Lt. A.T. ARLOTT resumed duties of Q.M.	
	11th-		Camp inspected by G.O.C. 50th Div. Lt. T.H. CORRIGAN and 2/Lt. G. O'B. HOURIHANE joined from U.K.	
	12th-		Training as usual.	
	13th-		Draft of 9 ORs joined	
	14th-		Inoculations T.A.B.	
	15th-		Battalion inspected by Army Commander.	
	16th-		Gas tests carried out by Abancourt Gas Officer.	
	17th-		Training as usual. LG firing on new range	

Army Form C. 2118

WAR DIARY
or
INTELLIGENCE SUMMARY
(Erase heading not required.)

2/R. Irish Fus.   Vol. 38 Page 2

Place	Date July	Hour	Summary of Events and Information	Remarks and references to Appendices
ABANCOURT	18th		Training as usual.	Dieppe 1/6 1/100,000
	19th		Route march 2 hours. Draft of 8 ORs rejoined from EGYPT	
	20th		Church Parades: C of E. R.C.	
	21st		Coy and Specialist training.	
	22nd		Disinfection of A coy B, C, D, training. Orders received at 13 to move to camp in vicinity of HAUDRICOURT. Draft of 13 f. 1 oRs rejoined from hospital. Settent in	
HAUDRICOURT	23rd		Specialist training, Construction of anti-landing trenches rifle range.	
	24th		-	
	25th		-	
	26th		-	- C - Coy cross country run	
	27th		- Lieut E. M. SMITH to Hospital afternoon very wet	- D - Coy cross country run
	28th		Church Services Coys & R.C. "A" Coy cross country run	
	29th		Training :- Specialist : coy recreational 2/Lt M J ARLOTT to Hospital	
			- "B" coy cross country run	
	30th		-	
	31st		- B+D Coys on 100x range	

J W E Johnson Lt Col

B.M.32/7.

To:- D. A. G.,
    3rd Echelon.

Herewith War Diary of 5th Royal Irish Fusiliers for month of August 1918.

2.9.1918.   H. Bowen.
                                              Captain,
                    Brigade Major, 48th Infantry Brigade.

Cover for Documents.

Nature of Enclosures.

CONFIDENTIAL

WAR DIARY

of

5TH (S) Bn R. IRISH Fus

From 1st Aug. to 31st Aug. 1918

(VOL. NO 39)

Notes, or Letters written.

WAR DIARY or INTELLIGENCE SUMMARY

Army Form C. 2118

5 R. Irish Fus. Vol. 39 Page 1.

Place	Date August	Hour	Summary of Events and Information	Remarks and references to Appendices
HAUDRICOURT	1st		Specialist coy training. Firing on range (100x)	B.7 Apr 16 1/10,000
	2nd		Hot day. General parade in afternoon. Lt. M.F. TYLOR, RAMC, joined for duty as R.M.O.	
	3rd		Wet day. Inspection by G.O.C. cancelled	
	4th		Church Parades: C of E & RC	
	5th		Inspection by G.O.C. 66th Div. Training in afternoon as usual. M. H. VITAL joined	
	6th		Training in Lewis gun specialist. Construction of range (700x) as interpreter	
	7th		Holiday: Battalion Sports	
	8th		Training as usual.	
	9th		— — — — 3 officers + 97 ORs proceeded on leave to U.K.	
	10th		— — — — 6 — 262 —	
	11th		Church service C of E & RC. 6 — 92 —	
	12th		Construction of 700x range and bombing kits. RCO's 1 Lt 1 OR class	
	13th		— — — — — — —	
	14th		— — — — — — -L/C G. Higgins to hospital	
	15th		— — — — — — —	
	16th		Firing on range: practice in bombing; L.G. firing	

WAR DIARY or INTELLIGENCE SUMMARY

5 R. Irish Fus. Vol. 39 Page 2

Army Form C. 2118

Place	Date	Hour	Summary of Events and Information	Remarks and references to Appendices
HAUDRICOURT	17th		Coy. and Gas Drill by cops.	
	18th		Church Parades Coy T. drill.	
	19th		firing on range.	
	20th		—	
	21st		—	
	22nd		Specialist Training	
	23rd		Preparations to move.	
	24th		Battalion entrained at ABANCOURT at 9.30 and moved to HOUDAIN detraining 8.45 pm. Marched to 16 Div. Reinforcement Camp.	Trains 44B
BOIS D'OLHAIN	25th		Settling in. Preparation made for absorbing 11th Bn. Roy Irish Fus.	
	26th		gentle preparations	
	27th		Bn. absorbed 11th Bn. Roy Irish Fus. moved to huts in NOEUX-LES-MINES. Lt. N.R REYNELL, Lt. P.I.R. SANDILANDS Lt. W.R LEWIS joined for duty. Capt. R.W. STEVENTON, Lt. H. ANDERSON, Lt. JOURDAIN taken on strength (on detachment. Lt. J.L. CREIGHTON. Lts. A.A.JAMES (Cor.Rogr), M.W.MOSS M.J. ARLOTT (in hospital) to bear for reporting. 150 O.Rs taken on strength.	
NOEUX LES MINES.				

1875 Wt. W593/826 1,000,000 4/15 J.B.C. & A. A.D.S.S./Forms/C. 2118.

WAR DIARY or INTELLIGENCE SUMMARY

Army Form C. 2118

5 R. Fus. Inl. Vol. 39 Page 3

Place	Date	Hour	Summary of Events and Information	Remarks and references to Appendices
NOEUX LES MINES	28th Aug		Relieving reconnaissance of the Reserve Line	France 44 B.
	29th		Battalion moved into Corps Reserve at BARLIN.	
BARLIN	30th		Settling in	
	31st		Bathing: Gas Inspection; Coy. platoon inspection, afternoon drills	
1st Sept				

M. Phene Major oc ppc
Comdg 5/4(S) Bn Roy Fusil Inn

CONFIDENTIAL

WAR DIARY

OF

5TH R. IRISH FUSILIERS

from 1st September to 30th September 1918

VOL No 40

Army Form C. 2118

WAR DIARY
or
INTELLIGENCE SUMMARY

(Erase heading not required.)

Vol 40 Pages

Place	Date	Hour	Summary of Events and Information	Remarks and references to Appendices
BARLIN	1st		Firing on REBREUVE Rifle range, 100x and 200x.	France 44 B
	2nd		Reconnaissance of defensive line. Platoon training.	
	3rd		Battalion Route March. Platoon Demonstration by Army Training Staff.	
	4th		Firing on Range. 300x; 5 rd. application; 5 rd. rapid application; 5 rd. rapid 10 rapid load with gas masks; 5 snapshots.	
	5th		Platoon training. Games.	
	6th		Bn. moved at 7 hrs. to Rutherick in NOEUX LES MINES.	
NOEUX LES MINES	7th		Settling in. Games.	
	8th		Church Services. 2nd Lt. R.E. (voluntary) Lt. J.H. DUNCAN joins; posted to C Coy.	
	9th		Firing on GAVION Range. Recruit Class under Lt. J.H. DOLAN	
	10th		Baths. Firing on REBREUVE Range by "A" & "C" Coys. Cancelled on account of wet.	
	11th		Baths. Platoon training. Open Warfare	
	12th		Demonstration by "C" Coy - Advancing by bounds. Platoon training. Coy drill	

WAR DIARY or INTELLIGENCE SUMMARY

Army Form C. 2118

Vol 40 Page 2

Place	Date	Hour	Summary of Events and Information	Remarks and references to Appendices
NOEUX LES MINES	13th		A Coy. "Bullet & Bayonet" Practice. Remdr. Platoon Training.	FRANCE 444 B.
	14th		B Coy. working half of 1.35. — — Recruits Class finish on march.	
	15th		Church Service C.g. B, R.b, & Res. 2 working parties on aerodrome at 6.30 a.m. and 7.30 p.m.	
	16th		Lewis Gunnery. C & A Coys. finish under L.g.O. Remdr. Platoon Training	
	17th		Tank Demonstration; all men not required for work attended. LT. COL. F.H.E.J.D HANSON & knapt: commanding 49	
	18th		Bn. moved to ANNEQUIN defences.	
ANNEQUIN	19th		Sy Pole. A Coy. occupied 4 huts of "Village Line"; B Coy. training. C & D Coys. working parties.	
	20th		B & D Coys. working; C Coy. Training — Platoon training L.g. arrangmt.	
	21st		B & C " D " A Coy. relieved in VILLAGE LINE	
			by 18th Gloster + billeted in ANNEQUIN.	
	22nd		A & B Coys. resting; C & D Coys. working. Divine Services; R.C. mass.	
	23rd	9.36 pm	A & C Coys. working. D Coy. relieves 18th Gloucesters in VILLAGE LINE	
	24th		B & C Coys. working A Coy. training; Platoon training	
	25th		A & C — — B — training	

WAR DIARY or INTELLIGENCE SUMMARY

Army Form C. 2118

Vol 40 Page 3

Place	Date Sept.	Hour	Summary of Events and Information	Remarks and references to Appendices
ANNEQUIN	26th		A + B Coys. working, C Coy training. Baths in ANNEQUIN.	44B NW
	27th		Bn. relieves 1/6 Somerset L.I. in Outpost line, A + C in front, B + D supporting. Posts at A.29.d.20.85, A.29.B.4.4, A.29.B.6.9, A.23.d.40.85.	LA BASSEE 44A NW1
INDIAN	28th		Reconnoitering patrol sent about 500 yds in front found ground unoccupied at 3 a.m. A.30.a.05.75. Casualties, 1 OR wounded.	
In the LINE	29th	3.15am 4.5 am	Siege M.G. + artillery fire. Posts established at A.30.c.75,85, A.30.a.2.3, A.24.c.15.30 and A.24.c.20.85. First, fourth, fifth without opposition. Second post under 2/Lt. H.A.J BERRY encountered and charged enemy patrol who fled leaving a M.G. and 10 rifles in our hands. Third post under Lt. J. CARROLL M.C. encountered strong opposition and established themselves short of objective. Heavy MG shelling in vicinity of AUCHY. Casualties 2 killed 3 wounded. A.30.c.15.85.	
	30th	9pm	Right forward post attacked on front, right and rear owing to post at A.30.c.10.50 being driven in. Lt. F.S SIMPSON held out supported by Lt. A.V. AMES from right support Coy, while Lt. R.W. CARR from right support platoon re-established post at A.30.c.10.50. 1 prisoner captured, M.G Sgt. 9, 370 Regt, 10 Frants Divs	

1875 Wt. W593/826 1,000,000 4/15 J.B.C. & A. A.D.S.S./Forms/C. 2118.

WAR DIARY
or
INTELLIGENCE SUMMARY

Army Form C. 2118

R. Fus. Bn. Vol No. Pages

Place	Date	Hour	Summary of Events and Information	Remarks and references to Appendices
Mellukin	Sept 30th	Middn 6.20am	Heavy bombardment of AUCHY and support positions. Enemy returning similar attack on left flank, an artillery (barrage) AUCHY ALLEY. No enemy attack developed. Patrols sent out at 3am to reconnoitre enemy wire along HAISNES ALLEY about 3.15 am. not hostile post at A.30.a.75.65 and was located along AUCHY ALLEY, encountered enemy at A.24.d.0.9.	LA BASSEE 44A NW1
		6.15 am	Reconnoitring patrol sent forward under cover of barrage, in conjunction with attack on left, reached point A.24.c.9.9 finding Irish wire and being fired up by M.G's.; and finding enemy posts established at A.30.a.25.95 and A.30.a.35.80.	
		3pm	2/Lt. R.W. CARR and 4 ORs worked up PEKIN ALLEY to A.30.a.75.00 bombing enemy bank to LA BASSEE - MULLOCH line wounding 1 and capturing 1 M.G.	
		10.30	Enemy patrol attempted to penetrate line between A.30.a.15.75 and A.24.B.1.3 but was driven back. Heavy shelling of AUCHY and Support positions. Casualties: 4 ORs killed. 14 wounded. 1 wounded at duty. 2/Lt J.M. Johnson. 2/Lt O.S. ? 1 missing.	

Vol 3

CONFIDENTIAL
WAR DIARY
OF
5TH (S) Bn. ROYAL IRISH FUSILIERS
FROM 1ST OCTOBER, 1918 to 31ST OCTOBER, 1918.

VOLUME No 41.

WAR DIARY
or
INTELLIGENCE SUMMARY

Army Form C. 2118

Vol 41 page

Place	Date	Hour	Summary of Events and Information	Remarks and references to Appendices
[illegible]	June 1	0300	Patrol proceeded along AUCHY ALLEY to enemy wire heard talking movement. Heavy shelling of support positions at intervals during day with H.E's 5.9 & 77mm, blue, green yellow cross.	LA BASSEE 44A NW.1
		1500	Patrol along PEKIN ALLEY found no enemy block at A.30.c.30.97 were fired on by about 30 men.	
		1900 -2300	Bn. relieved in Outpost Line by 22nd NORTHUMBERLAND FUSILIERS and moved into Brigade Reserve in CAMBRIN; B'd in VILLAGE LINE in LEWIS KEEP, MAISON ROUGE, DELHI and TOULOUSE on the right and KANDAHAR [illegible] LOUISBERG and MOULTAN on the left. A & C Coys in CAMBRIN MB, CAMBRIN LOCALITY COMMAND POST. Casualties :- 1 Or. killed, 6 wounded (actually 1 missing. 3 miles killed by shellfire in CAMBRIN.	
CAMBRIN	2nd	1300	A Coy moved up to RESERVE LINE to took PYRENEES, BOGNOR, LITTLE HAMPTON and MOUNTAIN KEEP coming under orders 18th [Pontreal?] Rifles. 1 Coy. 9 GLOUCESTERS in VILLAGE line Came in exchange to	
		1720	C Coy occupied posts in RESERVE LINE, BURBURY, WILSON'S TUNNEL, CUIDAD and SALAMANCA + Res. H.Q. b-BRADDELL POINT. A Coy reverted to Bn. for when Reconnaissance of forward areas [illegible]	
	3rd		GLOUCESTERS reverted to own Bn. training. Lt. B.R. LEWIS accidentally wounded by Grenade explosion	

WAR DIARY
INTELLIGENCE SUMMARY

Army Form C. 2118

Place	Date	Hour	Summary of Events and Information	Remarks and references to Appendices
BRADDELL POINT	4th		Further reconnaissance of forward areas & individual training. Bathing at ANNEQUIN. B.HQ. moved at 16.30 to ROBERTSON'S TUNNEL.	A. BRADELL ROBERTSON'S TUNNEL ANNEX 7.
ROBERTSON'S TUNNEL	5th		Battalion relieved 18th Scottish Rifles in SUPPORT LINE, B and D forward line, A and C in support. Bn. HQ at CITÉ DE DOUVRIN. Posn as follows:- B Coy :- H.Q. B.3.a.1.3, B.27.d.1.4, B.27.a.7.2 and H. 2.B.1.9 with HQ at B.26.b.31. D Coy:- B.21.a.9.6, B.15.a.2.5, B.15.b.8.5. and HQ wit 1 Platoon, B.15.c.2.3. A Coy:- B.26.c.9.5, B.26.a.3.3, B.15.b.2.7, B.25.d.4.8, HQ at B.25.B.2.0. C Coy:- VENDIN-DOUVRIN line from B.26.a.1.9 to B.19.a.9.9. 1 Platoon B.19.c.8.2. HQ. B.19.a.2.3.	
	6th		Reconnaissance of forward area.	
	7th		—	
	8th		— Improvement of positions	
	9th		Bn relieved by 18th Welsh Regt. + moved to Bde. in support in CAMBRIN.	

H. A. E. THUNDER Major

WAR DIARY or INTELLIGENCE SUMMARY

Army Form C. 2118

Vol 41 Page 3.

Place	Date Oct	Hour	Summary of Events and Information	Remarks and references to Appendices
CAMBRIN	10th		Settling in. Paying but 11783 Pte POLLOCK T. "A" Coy awarded M.M.	LA BASSEE 1/10,000.
	11th		Baths. Platoon Training. Close order & arms drill.	
	12th		Platoon & Company training.	
	13th		Church Parade. Close order drill. Musketry &c.	
	14th		A, B & D Coys. Rifles Rd. working parties. C Coy Musketry. Capt. W.A. BEATTIE M.C. & Lt. E.M. SMITH proceed on 7 days leave to U.K. to Course.	
	15th		Training; Outpost schemes; Musketry. Pro tem orders to be ready to move to CITÉ de DOUVRIN locality owing to Canal de HAUTE DEULE being crossed. 22365 Sgt. JONES G. awarded D.C.M.	
CITÉ DE DOUVRIN		18.00	Bn. moves to CITÉ DE DOUVRIN locality. Will Breakfast at DOUVRIN and Stew at HAISNES.	44 A 1/40,000.
BILLY	16th		Bn. moved 1000 to BILLY BERCLAU. H.Q, B.23 central, will B Coy to BRIQUETTE FACTORY, C.25 d.5.5; A & D in BERCLAU, B.19 central; C Coy. starts transport in BILLY. BAUVIN and PROVIN reconnoitred with a view to further advance. Lt. R. MAXWELL to Hospital.	
PROVIN	17th	07.45	Battalion moves to PROVIN, with 3 coys. in PROVIN; D Coy. in FOSSE 7.	
		16.00	C.15. d.3.3. and took over Forward Edge of Battle Zone. Bn. advanced to ANNOEULLIN B, D & HQ; C & A Coys. to CARNIN.	

WAR DIARY or INTELLIGENCE SUMMARY

Army Form C. 2118

Royal Fus[ilie]rs Vol. 41. Page 4.

Place	Date	Hour	Summary of Events and Information	Remarks and references to Appendices
ATTICHES	18th	0830	Bn. left ANNOEULLIN, picking up A + C Coys. at CARNIN and marched to ATTICHES, with C Coy. to PETIT ATTICHES. A. in ATTICHES, B. in MARTINSART and D. in WATTIESSART, arrived at 1430. Detained on the way by leading Bde. transport. Roads mined at every important junction, necessitating many detours.	44 A. 1/40,000.
	19th	0900	Scheme launched to PETIT ATTICHES & PETIT ATTICHES : Bn. HQ, O.M. Transport & MARTINSART. A Coy, moved to PETIT ATTICHES. B Coy. became Bde. in Reserve.	
	20th		Divine Service; Coy R. &c. pde.	
	21st	1020	Bn. moved to ENNEVLIN.	
ENNEVLIN	22nd		Division instructed to stand fast. Bathing, washing &c.	
	23rd		Washing; P.T. musketry	
	24th		Practice of Advance Guard formations	
	25th		" " "	
	26th		" " "	
	27th		Church parade; Coy to R.E. be pdes.	
	28th		Advance Guard formations	

Army Form C. 2118

WAR DIARY
or
INTELLIGENCE SUMMARY

(Erase heading not required.)

5th Royal Fusiliers   Vol. 41   Page 5

Place	Date	Hour	Summary of Events and Information	Remarks and references to Appendices
ENNEVELIN	Oct 29th		A, B & C: working on roads at GENECH (Sheet 44, A.15.b). Remainder of C, D. HQ ; bathing.	44 A 1/40,000
	30th		½ B, C & D working on roads at GENECH. A Coy. & remainder of B & C Coy. bathing.	
	31st		Advance Guard formation ; remainder of B & C Coy. bathing.	

W. Dickson
Lt. Col.
9/11/18 OC 5 Royal Fus

CONFIDENTIAL.

WAR DIARY

OF

5TH (S.) BN. ROYAL IRISH FUSILIERS.

FROM 1ST NOV. 1918 TO 30TH NOV. 1918

VOLUME No. 42.

Army Form C. 2118

WAR DIARY or INTELLIGENCE SUMMARY

(Erase heading not required.)

5th Royl Irish Fusiliers Vol. 42 Page 1

Place	Date Nov.	Hour	Summary of Events and Information	Remarks and references to Appendices
ENNEVELIN	1st		Inspection of kit, shoes etc. R.C. Service in Church.	44 A. 1/40,000
	2nd		A & D Coys - voted on new B.C. Coys training - Attaque Quards. Orders received to move to RUMES on 3rd.	
	3rd		Batalion marches to RUMES. Reconnaissance of FLORENT LINE.	
RUMES	4th		Further reconnaissance of FLORENT LINE. Settling in.	37 1/40,000
	5th		Reconnaissance of Outpost Line. Wet day; no work possible.	
	6th	1400	Bn. marches from RUMES; halts at TAINTIGNIES for tea; left TAINTIGNIES 1600 to relieve 34th London Regt. in the Outpostline. B - D in the line; A + C in support. HQ.1 LONGUE SAULT.	
Outpostline	7th	2145	Relief complete. Quiet night. Considerable shelling all day; H.E., green + yellow cross. Two explosions in TOURNAI at 1730 and one at 1400 in ANTOING.	
	8th		3 O.R. wounded At 2000 batt. of 3 Grenadiers on foot, but returned ordinary front. night of 7th/8th. B Coy relieved by B Coy 18th Scottish Rifles — marches to TAINTIGNIES. Relief complete 0400. 8th Capt. G. H. Golloghly RAMC.	
			Patrol under Lt. E. J. ECCLES found enemy clear of V. 13 t. A + C Coys ordered to send out reconnoitering patrols supported by fighting patrols 4-500 yards to occupy ground vacated by enemy.	

WAR DIARY or INTELLIGENCE SUMMARY

Army Form C. 2118

5th Royal Fus[iliers] ? Vol. 42 Page 2

Place	Date	Hour	Summary of Events and Information	Remarks and references to Appendices
Wulverghem	Mar 6	0800	Ground unoccupied 500 yds. infantry foot. Fighting patrols occupied line of posts established by reconnoitring patrols whoever ordered to push to Canal bank. Posts on line V.20.c.8.3 – V.20.a.5.5 – V.14.c.2.2 – V.13.a.8.6 approx. B Coy. Scottish Rifles ordered to advance in outpost. D Coy. occupied WARNAFFLES FARM and formed defensive flank till relieved by 55th Division (only).	line 37 1/40,0.00
		1200	Heavy MG fire from the Zonnie V.27.a.5.4 and from V.27.c.65.60, V.21.d. 48.55 and from Convent in V.21.b and church V.16.c. 6 m.g.s in houses. Guns apparently unable to hit same, but in houses in the Zonnie not barrage above the Zonnie V.20.d.0.8 with shrapnel but retaliated V.20.d.35.45, V.20 & 9.3, V.20.d.7.9 and V.14 &.6.3 which patrol worked forward to V.15 central.	
		1330	MG's active still hold up a heavy retaliatic checking advance.	
		1700 Dusk	Relief by Scottish Rifles commenced.	
		2000	Relief cancelled and the following operation substituted :– 18 Scot. Rif. & rei[nf] right of our line and 22nd Northumberland Fusilier to relief left : then Rev. Bros. to continue advance and cross the river.	
		2030 5th Div	(enemy) reported across the river. Bridges broken orders brought up from BRUYELLE and hulks over bridge had formed A Coy. to conduct the operation order previously received.	

WAR DIARY or INTELLIGENCE SUMMARY

5th Royal Fus[ilier]s Indian? Vol. H 2 Page 3

Army Form C. 2118

Place	Date	Hour	Summary of Events and Information	Remarks and references to Appendices
	8th	1200	A Coy. boat party relieved by 18th Sco. Rif. who proceed with operation. Enemy had apparently withdrawn his rearguard after dark.	37. 1/40,000
	9th	0300	A Coy. completely relieved & marches to LONGUE SAULT. (V.22.c) C.D. relieved later into morning and marches to ST. MAUR. (V.17.b) Sco. Rif. & Northumberland Fusiliers crossed river without opposition. Rooftrops? Bridgeheads. Casualties:- 1 O.R. killed. 5 O.R. wounded.	
		1700	"B" Echelon, Gun Stores Transport moved to LONGUE SAULT.	
	10th		Bn. moved to billets in ANTOING.	
ANTOING	11th	0800	Settled in billets. Hostilities ceased at 1100. Parade to receive congratulations and thanks of Brig. Gen. Comd.g 48 Inf. Bde. Inventories.	
	12th	-	Company Ceremonial Drill.	
	13th	-	— Lieut. A.V. AMES to U.K. (to Board of Trade).	
	14th	-	—	
	15th		Bn. marched to GUIGNIES.	
Luis [of] March	16th		March continued to COBRIEUX. 2 additional q.d. began & Lorry allowed for more 44.. q.d. began withdrawn after move.	44. 1/40,000

Army Form C. 2118

WAR DIARY
or
INTELLIGENCE SUMMARY
(Erase heading not required.)

Royal Irish Fusiliers Vol. 42, Page 4.

Place	Date	Hour	Summary of Events and Information	Remarks and references to Appendices
MERIGNIES AREA K.6.T.12., L.1.7.8.	17th		March continued to MERIGNIES area. Motor lorry not allowed for this journey. HQ & Sig: Château de Broux, L.1.7.d.; HQ personnel at NOUVEAU JEU, L.1.1.d.; Stores, A & B Coys - MERIGNIES; C Coy - LA ROSIERE; D Coy - LA VERDERIE.	4.4.A 1/40,000
	18th		Settling in	
	19th		Company Drill. Rev. J.J. DOYLE joined	
	20th		" ; Coys. bathing. Lt. T.F. ESPIE & Lt. J.C. NICOLLS joined; posted to B Coy.	
	21st		" ; Blankets disinfected. Rev. K.D. DELANEY reported.	
	22nd		Battalion Ceremonial Drill. Rev. J.J. DOYLE left.	
	23rd		Coy. & Arthur of Coy. Cmdrs. for Kit inspection. Cross-country walk.	
	24th		Divine Service - R.C. & Pros.	
	25th		Platoon Specialist training. Capt. P.N. OWEN RANE to U.K. interchange of contract. Capt. D.S. BADENOCH RANE joined	
	26th		" Lt. CLENDINNING, Lt. J.A. CHAMBERS, Lt. W. MERCIER & Lt. P.L. DAVIS joined; posted to A, B, C, D respectively.	
	27th		Battalion Route March. Transport Turnout Competition	

Army Form C. 2118

WAR DIARY
or
INTELLIGENCE SUMMARY

(Erase heading not required.)

2nd Royal Irish Regt.   Vol. 42 Page 5

Instructions regarding War Diaries and Intelligence Summaries are contained in F. S. Regs., Part II. and the Staff Manual respectively. Title Pages will be prepared in manuscript.

Place	Date	Hour	Summary of Events and Information	Remarks and references to Appendices
HERGNIES	28th		Preparations for move. Lt. G.E. CHIPLIN joined; posted to "B"Coy.	44 A 1/40,000
	29th		Battalion moved to TEMPLEUVE.	
TEMPLEUVE	30th		Bathing. Games.	

F.W.B. Johnston Lt.
Lt & Adjt.

[signature]
Commanding

CONFIDENTIAL

WAR DIARY

of

5TH (S) BN ROYAL IRISH FUSILIERS

FROM 1ST DEC 1918 to 31ST DEC. 1918

VOLUME No 43

PAGES 1-2.

Army Form C. 2118

WAR DIARY
or
INTELLIGENCE SUMMARY

(Erase heading not required.)

5th Royal Irish Fusiliers   Vol. 43. Page 1.

Instructions regarding War Diaries and Intelligence Summaries are contained in F.S. Regs., Part II. and the Staff Manual respectively. Title Pages will be prepared in manuscript.

Place	Date	Hour	Summary of Events and Information	Remarks and references to Appendices
TEMPLEUVE	1st	–	Church Services. Coy. P.E., Rev. Wks.	44 A. 1/40,000.
	2nd	–	Cleaning the vicinity of billets, making baths re.	
	3rd	–	Platoon specialist training.	
	4th	–	Coy. Ceremonial Drill.	
	5th	–	Brigade Route March.	
	6th	–	Bn. Ceremonial Drill.	
	7th	–	Interior Economy. Kit inspections re.	
	8th	–	Divine Service. Coy E., R.E., Rev. Wks.	
	9th	–	Coy. at disposal of Coy. Commanders. Baths.	
	10th	–	Bn. Ceremonial Drill.	
	11th	–	Coys. at disposal of Coy. Cmdrs. 3 O.Rs. (miners) to U.K.	
	12th	–	Brigade Ceremonial Drill cancelled owing to weather. 44 O.R. (miners) to U.K.	
	13th	–	Bn. Route March. 7 O.R. (miners to U.K.)	
	14th	–	Indian grooms, Inspection Baths. 4 O.R. (miners) to U.K.	
	15th	–	Divine Service. Coy. R., Rev. Wks.	
	16th	–	Coys at disposal O.C. Coy. Cmdrs. for Ceremonial Drill.	
	17th	–	Battn. Ceremonial Drill. 5 O.R. (miners) to U.K.	

WAR DIARY or INTELLIGENCE SUMMARY

Army Form C. 2118

5th Royal Irish Fusiliers Vol #3 Page 2

Place	Date	Hour	Summary of Events and Information	Remarks and references to Appendices
TEMPLEUVE	Dec 1918			
	18th		Coys. at disposal of Coy. Comdrs. for P.T., Platoon + Spec. training	4½
	19th		Brigade Ceremonial Drill cancelled on account of weather. Bn. Route March held instead.	1/40000
	20th		Coys. at disposal of Coy. Comdrs.	
	21st		Interior economy. Kit Inspection. Baths.	
	22nd		Divine Services. C of E., R.C. Pres-tern. 1 O.R. (miner) to U.K.	
	23rd		Coys. at disposal of Coy. Comdrs for Platoon + Spec. traing.	
	24th		Cleaning + decorating billets for Xmas Day. R.C. Midnight Mass.	
	25th		Christmas Day. Divine Services. C of E., R.C., Pres. etc.	
	26th		General holiday. Transport Brigade.	
	27th		Physical Drill + Games in billets.	
	28th		Baths. Interior Economy. Kit Inspection. 20 O.R. to U.K. — one funeral man, men on compassionate	
	29th		Divine Services C of E., R.C. Pres. usu. 11 O.R. Lionfard Details + 1 Long Service man	
	30th		Coys. at disposal of Coy. Comdr. to U.K.	
	31st		Battalion Parade: Route March.	

John M Mays
Lieut & Adjutant

H.S. Sweeting
Major Commdg
5th Royal Irish Fusrs.

CONFIDENTIAL F.M.

War Diary

of

5th (S) Bn. Royal Irish Fusiliers

from January 1st 1919 to January 31st 1919

Volume 44

CONFIDENTIAL

Army Form C. 2118

WAR DIARY
or
INTELLIGENCE SUMMARY

(Erase heading not required.)

2nd Royal Irish Fusiliers Vol. 44 Page 1.

Place	Date	Hour	Summary of Events and Information	Remarks and references to Appendices
TEMPLEMORE	Jan. 1		Coys. at disposal of Coy. Cmdrs. Church Service. Cyfs. Ptl.	44 A
	2		Sports & games	
	3		" "	
	4		" "	
	5		Baths. Inspection of kits etc.	
	5		Church parades. Coy. P.T. etc.	9 O.Rs. demobilised
	6		Delousing & Baths	
	7		Battalion Route March	
	8		B.P.T., Musketry etc	
	9		" "	
	10		Battalion Ceremonial drill	
	11		Baths. Interior Economy	
	12 F		Church Parades. Duties	2 O.Rs. demobilised
	13		Duties: all available men on works and guards.	29 " "
	14		" "	
	15		" "	
	16		" "	

Army Form C. 2118.

WAR DIARY
or
INTELLIGENCE SUMMARY.

(Erase heading not required.)

Vol. 44 Page 2

3 Royal Fusiliers

Instructions regarding War Diaries and Intelligence Summaries are contained in F. S. Regs., Part II. and the Staff Manual respectively. Title pages will be prepared in manuscript.

Place	Date	Hour	Summary of Events and Information	Remarks and references to Appendices
TEMPLEUVE	17		Duly Bn. training, baths, parades	4 4 A
	18		—	11/20,000
	19		Church parade; Cy E R.E. from Lt. J.A. CHAMBERS & 4 O.R.s demobilised.	
	20		Coy. at disposal of Coy. Cmdr. A.W.M. MOORE to Hospital. Sports, games — 2 O.R. demobilised	
	21		—	
	22		—	
	23		Lectire Battalion parade; presentation of Divisional Rugbies Certificates	
	24		Coy at disposal Coy cmdr	
	25		Baths etc. Lt. R.W. CARR and 3 O.R. demobilised	
	26		Church Parade Cy E. R.E. Lt. D.M. SMITH, Lt. T.E. DILNOT and 7 O.R.s demobilised.	
	27		Train fires on —	
	28		Coy. at disposal of Coy. cmdr. Working parties. Instructions: POR's demobilised	
	29		—	8 O.R.s demobilised
			Movements. 5 O.R. demobilised	

Army Form C. 2118.

WAR DIARY
or
INTELLIGENCE SUMMARY.

Instructions regarding War Diaries and Intelligence Summaries are contained in F. S. Regs., Part II. and the Staff Manual respectively. Title pages will be prepared in manuscript.

5 Royal Irish Fusiliers (Egase heading not required.)   Vol. 44 Page 3.

Place	Date	Hour	Summary of Events and Information	Remarks and references to Appendices
TEMPLEUVE	Jan 30		Coy. at disposal of Gp. Cmdr. working parties.	4 4 A 1/40,000
	31		—	
			—	
Bourghelles			H.S. Sweeting Major.	

Confidential

War Diary

of

5th (S) Bn. Royal Irish Fusiliers

From February 1st 1919 To February 28th 1919

Volume No. 45

WAR DIARY or INTELLIGENCE SUMMARY

Army Form C. 2118.

Vol. 45 page 1.

Place	Date	Hour	Summary of Events and Information	Remarks and references to Appendices
TEMPLEUVE	1st		Baths - working parties.	44 A
	2nd		Coal fatigues. Visit from H.R.H. The Prince of Wales (informal)	1/40000
	3rd		Release of presentation of colours. LT. F.C.BERNARD, LT. T.H.CORRIGAN + 34 O.Rs. demobilised.	
	4th		1 O.R. demobilised	
	5th		King's Colour presented to the Battalion by Corps Commander. H.E. Sir Arthur HOLLAND. 1 O.R. demobilised	
	6th		Coys. at disposal of Coy. Cmdrs. L. T.F.ESPIE died while on leave in UK 13 OR	
	7th		—	
	8th		Baths. Interior Economy. Coal fatigue. 7/Lt. H.A.J.BERRY to UK. prior to joining R.A.F.	
	9th		Church Service. C.B. No 1. Parade. 15 O.Rs. demobilised.	
	10th		Working parties. Coal fatigue. 16 "	
	11th		— 2/Lt. W.L.DIX evacuated to UK	
	12th		— Sports.	
	13th		— 17 O.Rs. demobilised.	

WAR DIARY or INTELLIGENCE SUMMARY

Army Form C. 2118.

5th Royal Irish Fusiliers

Place	Date	Hour	Summary of Events and Information	Remarks and references to Appendices
TEMPLEMORE	14th		Working parties & guards. 18 ORs demobilized	Issue 2 W A
	15th		Guards. 19 ORs demobilized	
	16th		Church Service Cof E. RCs rec'd voluntary Guards. 37 ORs demobilized.	1/140.00 O. 1/15 O'C. Prevailed on R.C. Presentation to O.C. Applied Course 22nd 8.30.
	17th		Guards. 16 ORs demobilized	
	18th		Guards.	
	19th		14 ORs demobilized.	
	20th		Working parties 20 ORs demobilized	
	21st		" 6 ORs demobilized	
	22nd		" 39 ORs demobilized	
	23rd		" 28 ORs demobilized	
	24th		" Sgt Selby transferred to 2nd Bedfords	
	25th		Working Parties & Guards	
	26th		" 5 ORs demobilized	
	27th			
	28		5 ORs demobilized	

J.K.E. Johnson Ll.Col
Comd'g 5 O.R. Irish Fus

Confidential

War Diary

of

5th (S) Bn Royal Irish Fusiliers

from March 1st 1919 to March 31st 1919

Volume No 46.

Army Form C. 2118.

WAR DIARY
or
INTELLIGENCE SUMMARY.
(Erase heading not required.)

Vol 46 Page 1

5th Royal Irish Fusiliers

Place	Date	Hour	Summary of Events and Information	Remarks and references to Appendices
Templeuve	March 1st		Packing of Battalion Equipment, relieved will G.1093	A/4 1 210.000
	2nd		Church Service (voluntary) Coys. R.E. then	
	3rd		Packing of equipment, preparation to move	
	4th		-	
	5th		BARROSA DAY. Holiday.	
	6th		Packing of equipment.	
	7th		-	
	8th		7 O.R. demobilised	
	9th		Church Service (voluntary) Coys. R.E.	
	10th		Packing of equipment. 2 O.R. joined	
	11th		-	
	12th		-	
	13th		3 O.R. demobilised	
	14th		-	

WAR DIARY
or
INTELLIGENCE SUMMARY.

Army Form C. 2118.

5 Royal Irish Fusiliers Vol 46 /pg 2

Place	Date	Hour	Summary of Events and Information	Remarks and references to Appendices
TEMPLEUVE	15th		Packing of equipment	44A
	16th		Divine Service (Voluntary) C of E. R.C. 2 officers (Lt L.R. MUIRHEAD + Lt P.E. HARM) 1/40000	
	17th		ST PATRICK'S DAY. Holiday. Parade & distribution of Shamrock	
	18th		Packing of Equipment. Lt R.V. JACKSON to 275 P.O.W. Coy 10th London	
	19th		Working party of 10 Bde. at Station	
	20th		-	
	21st		-	
	22nd		- Lt H. ANDERSON (A.D.HQ) demobilized. Administrative	
	23rd		Church Service (Vol.) R.C. to join 7/8 R. Innis. Fus. on march of orders. Lt. T. GERAGHTY rec to top	
	24th		Packing of equipment	
	25th		Checking of equipment by A.D.O.S. I Corps. Lt J. GLENDINNING and 31 ORs Bde. attached to 16 Bde. Group. demobilized.	
	26th		Final instructions received for disposal of Army of Occupation offices man Lt. F.S. SIMPSON evacuated to UK	

WAR DIARY
or
INTELLIGENCE SUMMARY.

Army Form C. 2118.

5th Royal Irish Fusiliers Vol. 46 Page 3.

Place	Date	Hour	Summary of Events and Information	Remarks and references to Appendices
TEMPLEUVE	27th		Col. W.A. BEATTIE M.C., CAPT. D.T. FIGGIS, Lt. H.B. REYNELL, 2/Lt's T.J. GALLAGHER, J. THORNTON, L. WARD DCM, J. CARROLL M.C., P/T. CATER, P.L. DAVIS, G.E. CHIPLIN, J.C.G. NICHOLLS and 39 ORs for Army of Occupation proceed via St ANDRÉ to join 1/8th Royal Inniskilling Fusiliers at BOULOGNE.	46 A 1/69000
	28th		Usual Routine	
	29th		h/Cn F.W.E. JOHNSON having proceeded on leave to UK MAJOR M.S. SWEETING assumed command	
	30th		Capt. R.McEWAN M.C., Lt. R.J. STRANGER, Maj. 2/Lt. W. MERCIER and 6 ORs demobilised	
	31st		Usual Routine	

M.S. Sweeting

W Pichon

Confidential

War Diary

of

5th (S) Bn. Royal Irish Fusiliers

from 1st April 1919 to 30th April 1919

Volume No. 47

Army Form C. 2118.

WAR DIARY
or
INTELLIGENCE SUMMARY.   Vol 47 Page 1

2 R. Irish Rgt.

(Erase heading not required.)

Place	Date	Hour	Summary of Events and Information	Remarks and references to Appendices
TEMPLEUVE (NORD)	1 Feb		Usual Routine	AAA A 1/40,000
	2			
	3			
	4			
	5		Church Service. R.C. & P/c.	
	6		Fatigue parts of 5 men found	
	7		do	
	8th		do	
	9th		do	
	10th			
	11th			
	12th		R.C. Service	
	13th		Fatigue parts	
	14th			
	15th		Usual Duties	
	16th			

Lt. J.H. Duncan – 2 o/c Anchiges

Army Form C. 2118.

WAR DIARY
or
INTELLIGENCE SUMMARY.

Vol. 47 page 1

(Erase heading not required.)

6 R Irish Fus

Place	Date	Hour	Summary of Events and Information	Remarks and references to Appendices
TEMPLEUVE (NORD)	17		Usual routine	44 A 1/10,000
	18		" "	
	19		R.C. Service	
	20		Usual routine	
	21		" "	
	22		" "	
	23		" "	
	24		" "	
	25		" "	
	26		R.C. Service	
	27		Usual Routine	
	28		" "	
	29		" "	
	30		" "	

Confidential.

War Diary

of

5th (S) Bn. Royal Irish Fusiliers.
from 1/5/19 to 31/5/19.

Volume No. 48

WAR DIARY or INTELLIGENCE SUMMARY

Army Form C. 2118.

5th R. Irish Regt. Vol. 48 Page 10

Place	Date	Hour	Summary of Events and Information	Remarks and references to Appendices
TEMPLEUVE (NORD)	May 1st		Usual Routine. Lieut. E.J. ECCLES demobilized.	France Sheet A 1/40,000
	2nd		"	
	3rd		Lt.Col. F.W.E. JOHNSON DSO resumed command of 16 Div. Group.	
	4th		R.C. Service	
	5th		Working party of 5 ORs supplied daily.	
	6th			
	7th		Capt. G.C. KIRKLAND + 4 ORs demobilized	
	8th		Sgt. R. Peare & 7/8 R. Irish Regt.	
	9th		7 ORs demobilized	
	10th			
	12th		1 OR	
	13th		2 ORs (deserters) rejoined	
	16th		2 ORs sent to join Army of Occupation – 5th R. Irish Regt.	
	18th		Major H.S. SWEETING demobilized. 4 ORs to Army of Occupation – 5th R. Irish Regt	
	23rd		Capt. H.E. SHEPPARD proceeded to join No 15 A.O.D. ROUXMESNIL.	
	28th		Orders received that Bn. will entrain for DUNKIRK on 31st. 2 ORs to 5 R. Irish Regt.	
	30th	1630	Orders received to entrain forthwith. Entraining commenced 1330.	
			Moved 15.50. NCOs left behind attached to 5th S.L.I. Remained strength 3 & 25.	
	31st		Arrived DUNKIRK 0100. Detained DUNKIRK 0100. Delowed moved to N°3 Camp, MARDYCK.	
MARDYCK				

F.W.E. Johnson Lt.Col.
Comd. 5 R. Irish Fus.

CONFIDENTIAL.

WAR DIARY

OF

5th (S.) Bn. Royal Irish Fusiliers

from 1st June 1919 to 9th June 1919.

Vol. 49.

Army Form C. 2118.

WAR DIARY
or
INTELLIGENCE SUMMARY.
(Erase heading not required.)

Vol HQ Page 1

Instructions regarding War Diaries and Intelligence Summaries are contained in F. S. Regs., Part II. and the Staff Manual respectively. Title pages will be prepared in manuscript. 5th Royal Irish Fusiliers

Place	Date June	Hour	Summary of Events and Information	Remarks and references to Appendices
MARDYCK	1st		Preparation for move.	
	2nd		Adv: party from HQ. to load vehicle: 4 F.F. (Wagons Loaded)	
	3rd	0800	Remainder of vehicles loaded on S.S. CLUTHA.	
		1200	Rank: embarked on S.S. MICHAEL SIDOROV C/o baggage party on S.S. CLUTHA	
		1400	SOUTHAMPTON	
	4th	0500	Disembarked. S.S. CLUTHA arrived about 0900	
SOUTHAMPTON		1300	Unloading Commenced, and at 1600 loaded entrain commenced	
		2000	Train left for GEORGETOWN	
	5th		Arrived GEORGETOWN 1830, having travelled via YORK, NEWCASTLE and EDINBURGH.	
GEORGETOWN	6th		From headquarters personnel despatches for demobilisation	
PREES HEATH	7th		Colours + 1st Reinforcement arrived at PREES HEATH at 1600 and left at 1730 for FLEETWOOD — BELFAST — x S.S. DUKE OF ARGYLL.	
BELFAST	8th		Colours arrive 0700	
	9th		Colours left for ARMAGH 0750. Arrived at ARMAGH CATHEDRAL 0750.	

b/Buchan

J.H.E. Johnson Lt-Colonel
Comdg 5th S.I.B. "R" Irish Fus.

www.ingramcontent.com/pod-product-compliance
Lightning Source LLC
Chambersburg PA
CBHW081452160426
43193CB00013B/2457